Adobe Acrobat DC
Keyboard Shortcuts

By

U. C-Abel Books.

All Rights Reserved

First Edition: 2017

ISBN-13: 978-1543228427
ISBN-10: 1543228429

Published by U. C-Abel Books.

Table of Contents

Acknowledgement.

All thanks to God Almighty for enabling us to bring this work to this point. He is a wonder indeed.

We want to specially appreciate the great company called Adobe Systems Inc. for their hard work and style of reasoning when it comes to providing the public with helpful programs and resources, and for helping us with some of the tips and keyboard shortcuts included in this book.

Dedication

We dedicate this book to every user of Adobe Acrobat DC.

Introduction.

After thinking of how to help computer users become more productive in their operation of computers and various fields, it came to our knowledge that there is a smart option many computer users ignore easily and that part has a high yielding capacity that is known to just few people.

We went into a deep research to broaden our knowledge of key combination and found it very helpful, then we started this series "Shortcut Matters" including tips, techniques, keyboard shortcuts, and packaging the title in a way it will attract readers and get a high rating class.

As people who love keyboard shortcuts we treat each topic plainly in an easy-to-read way even to the understanding of a lay man.

Relax and make your mind ready for learning as we go.

How We Began.

We enjoy using shortcuts because they set us on a high plane that astonishes people around us when we work with them. As wonderful shortcuts users, the worst eyesore we witness in computer operation is to see somebody sluggishly struggling to execute a task through mouse usage when in actual sense shortcuts will help to save that person time. Most people have asked us to help them with a list of keyboard shortcuts that can make them work as smartly as we do and that drove us into research to broaden our knowledge and truly help them as they demanded, that is the reason for the existence of this book. It is a great tool for lovers of shortcuts, and those who want to join the group.

Most times the things we love don't come by easily. It is our love for keyboard shortcuts that made us to bear long sleepless nights like owls just to make sure we get the best out of it, and it is the best we got that we are sharing with you in this book. You cannot be the same at computing after reading this book. The time you entrusted to our care is an expensive possession and we promise not to mess it up.

Thank you.

What to Know Before You Begin.

General Notes.

1. Most of the keyboard shortcuts you will see in this book refer to the U.S. keyboard layout. Keys for other layouts might not correspond exactly to the keys on a U.S. keyboard. Keyboard shortcuts for laptop computers might also differ.

2. It is important to note that when using shortcuts to perform any command, you should make sure the target area is active, if not, you may get a wrong result. Example, if you want to highlight all texts you must make sure the text field is active and if an object, make sure the object area is active. The active area is always known by the location where the cursor of your computer blinks.

3. On a Mac keyboard, the Command key is denoted with the ⌘ symbol.

4. If a function key doesn't work on your Mac as you expect it to, press the Fn key in addition to the function key. If you don't want to press the Fn key every time, you can change your Apple system preferences.

5. The plus (+) sign that comes in the middle of keyboard shortcuts simply means the keys are

meant to be combined or held down together not to be added as one of the shortcut keys. In a case where plus sign is needed; it will be duplicated (++).

6. Many keyboards assign special functions to function keys, by default. To use the function key for other purposes, you have to press Fn+the function key.

7. For keyboard shortcuts in which you press one key immediately followed by another key, the keys are separated by a comma (,).

8. It is also important to note that the keyboard shortcuts, tips, and techniques listed in this book are for users of Adobe Acrobat DC.

9. To get more information on this title visit ucabelbooks.wordpress.com and search the site using keywords related to it.

10. Our chief website is under construction.

Some Short Forms You Will Find in This Book and Their Full Meaning.

Here are short forms used in this Adobe Acrobat DC Keyboard Shortcuts book and their full meaning.

1. Win   -   Windows logo key
2. Tab   -   Tabulate Key
3. Shft   -   Shift Key
4. Prt sc   -   Print Screen
5. Num Lock   -   Number Lock Key
6. F   -   Function Key
7. Esc   -   Escape Key
8. Ctrl   -   Control Key
9. Caps Lock -   Caps Lock Key
10. Alt   -   Alternate Key

CHAPTER 1.

Fundamental Knowledge of Keyboard Shortcuts.

Without the existence of the keyboard, there wouldn't have been anything like keyboard shortcuts so in this chapter we will learn a little about the computer keyboard before moving to keyboard shortcuts.

1. Definition of Computer Keyboard.

This is an input device that is used to send data to computer memory.

Sketch of a Keyboard

1.1 Types of Keyboard.

i. Standard (Basic) Keyboard.
ii. Enhanced (Extended) Keyboard.

i. **Standard Keyboard:** This is a keyboard designed during the 1800s for mechanical typewriters with just 10 function keys (F keys) placed at the left side of it.

ii. **Enhanced Keyboard:** This is the current 101 to 102-key keyboard that is included in almost all the personal computers (PCs) of nowadays, which has 12 function keys, usually at the top side of it.

Function Keys

Numeric Keys

Alphabetic keys

1.2 Segments of the keyboard

- Numeric keys.
- Alphabetic keys.
- Punctuation keys.
- Windows Logo key.
- Function keys.
- Special keys.

Numeric Keys: Numeric keys are keys with numbers from **0 - 9**.

Alphabetic Keys: These are keys that have alphabets on them, ranging from **A** to **Z**.

Punctuation Keys: These are keys of the keyboard used for punctuation, examples include comma, full stop, colon, question marks, hyphen, etc.

Windows Logo Key: A key on Microsoft Computer keyboard with its logo displayed on it. Search for this ⊞ on your keyboard.

Apple Key: This also known as Command key is a modifier key that you can find on an Apple keyboard. It usually has the image of an apple or command logo on it. Search for this on your Apple keyboard

Function Keys: These are keys that have **F** on them which are usually combined with other keys. They are F1 - F12, and are also in the class called *Special Keys*.

Special Keys: These are keys that perform special functions. They include: Tab, Ctrl, Caps lock, Insert, Prt sc, alt gr, Shift, Home, Num lock, Esc, and many others. Special keys differ according to the type of computer involved. In some keyboard layout, especially laptops, the keys that turn the speaker on/off, the one that increases/decreases volume, the key that turns the computer Wifi on/off are also special keys.

Other Special Keys Worthy of Note.

Enter Key: This is located at the right-hand corner of most keyboards. It is used to send messages to the computer to execute commands, in most cases it is used to mean "Ok" or "Go".

Escape Key (ESC): This is the first key on the upper left of most keyboards. It is used to cancel routines, close menus and select options such as **Save** according to circumstances.

Control Key (CTRL): It is located on the bottom row of the left and right hand side of the keyboard. They also work with the function keys to execute commands using Keyboard shortcuts (key combinations).

Alternate Key (ALT): It is located on the bottom row also of some keyboard, very close to the CTRL key on both side of the keyboard. It enables many editing functions to be accomplished by using some keystroke combinations on the keyboard.

Shift Key: This adds to the roles of function keys. In addition, it enables the use of alternative function of a particular button (key), especially, those with more than one function on a key. E.g. use of capital letters, symbols, and numbers.

1.3. Selecting/Highlighting With Keyboard.

This is a highlighting method or style where data is selected using the computer keyboard instead of a computer mouse.

To do this:

- Move your cursor to the text or object you want to highlight, make sure that area is active,
- Hold down the shift key with one finger,
- Then use another finger to move the arrow key that points to the direction you want to highlight.

1.4 The Operating Modes Of The Keyboard.

Just like the computer mouse, keyboard has two operating modes. The two modes are Text Entering Mode and Command Mode.

a.   **Text Entering Mode:** this mode gives the operator/user the opportunity to type text.
b.   **Command Mode:** this is used to command the operating system/software/application to execute commands in certain ways.

2. Ways To Improve In Your Typing Skill.

1. Put Your Eyes Off The Keyboard.

This is the aspect of keyboard usage that many don't find funny because they always ask. "How can I put my eyes off the keyboard when I am running away from the occurrence of errors on my file?" My aim is to be fast, is this not going to slow me down?

Of course, there will be errors and at the same time your speed will slow down but the motive behind the introduction to this method is to make you faster than you are. Looking at your keyboard while you type can make you get a sore neck, it is better you learn to touch type because the more you type with your eyes fixed on the screen instead of the keyboard, the faster you become.

An alternative to keeping your eyes off your keyboard is to use the *"Das Keyboard Ultimate"*.

2. Errors Challenge You

It is better to fail than to not try at all. Not trying at all is an attribute of the weak and lazybones. When you make mistakes, try again because errors are opportunities for improvement.

3. Good Posture (Position Yourself Well).

Do not adopt an awkward position while typing. You should get everything on your desk organized or arranged before sitting to type. Your posture while typing contributes to your speed and productivity.

4. Practice

Here is the conclusion of everything said above. You have to practice your shortcuts constantly. The practice alone is a way of improvement. "Practice brings improvement". Practice always.

2.1 Software That Will Help You Improve Your Typing Skill.

There are several Software programs for typing that both kids and adults can use for their typing skill. Here is a list of software that can help you improve in your typing: Mavis Beacon, Typing Instructor, Mucky Typing Adventure, Rapid Tying Tutor, Letter Chase Tying Tutor, Alice Touch Typing Tutor and many more. Personally, I love Mavis Beacon.

To learn typing using MAVIS BEACON, install Mavis Beacon software to your computer, start with keyboard lesson, then move to games. Games like **_Penguin Crossing, Creature Lab_**, or **_Space Junk_** will help you become a professional in typing. Typing and keyboard shortcuts work hand-in-hand.

Sketch of a computer mouse

Right Mouse button

Scroll button

Left Mouse button

3. Mouse:

This is an oval-shaped portable input device with three buttons for scrolling, left clicking, and right clicking that enables work to be done effectively on a computer. The plural form of mouse is mice.

3.1 Types of Computer Mouse

- Mechanical Mouse.
- Optical Mechanical Mouse (Optomechanical).
- Laser Mouse.
- Optical Mouse.

- BlueTrack Mouse.

3.2 Forms of Clicking:

Left Clicking: This is the process of clicking the left side button of the mouse. It can also be called *clicking* without the addition of *left*.

Right Clicking: It is the process of clicking the right side button of a computer mouse.

Double Clicking: It is the process of clicking the left side button two times (twice) and immediately.

Triple Clicking: It is the process of clicking the left side button three times (thrice) and immediately.

Double clicking is used to select a word while triple clicking is used to select a sentence or paragraph.

Scroll Button: It is the little key attached to the mouse that looks like a tiny wheel. It takes you up and down a page when moved.

3.3 Mouse Pad: This is a small soft mat that is placed under the mouse to make it have a free movement.

3.4 Laptop Mouse Touchpad

This unlike the mouse we explained above is not external, rather it is inbuilt (comes with the laptop computer). With the presence of a laptop mouse touchpad, an external mouse is not needed to use a laptop, except in a case where it is malfunctioning or the operator prefers to use external one for some reasons.

The laptop mouse touchpad is usually positioned at the end of the keyboard section of a laptop computer. It is rectangular in shape with two buttons positioned below it. The two buttons/keys are used for left and right clicking just like the external mouse. Some laptops come with four mouse keys. Two placed above the mouse for left and right clicking and two other keys placed below it for the same function.

4. Definition Of Keyboard Shortcuts.

Keyboard shortcuts are defined as a series of keys, most times with combination that execute tasks which typically involve the use of mouse or other input devices.

5. Why You Should Use Shortcuts.

1. One may not be able to use a computer mouse easily because of disability or pain.

2. One may not be able to see the mouse pointer as a result of vision impairment, in such case what will the person do? The answer is SHORTCUT.

3. Research has made it known that Extensive mouse usage is related to Repetitive Syndrome Injury (RSI) greatly than the use of keyboard.

4. Keyboard shortcuts speed up computer users, making learning them a worthwhile effort.

5. When performing a job that requires precision, it is wise that you use the keyboard instead of mouse, for instance, if you are dealing with Text Editing, it is better you handle it using keyboard shortcuts than spending more time doing it with your computer mouse alone.

6. Studies calculate that using keyboard shortcuts allows working 10 times faster than working with the mouse. The time you spend looking for the mouse and then getting the cursor to the position you want is lost! Reducing your work duration by 10 times gives you greater results.

5.1 Ways To Become A Lover Of Shortcuts.

1. Always have the urge to learn new shortcut keys associated with the programs you use.
2. Be happy whenever you learn a new shortcut.
3. Try as much as you can to apply the new shortcuts you learnt.

4. Always bear it in mind that learning new shortcuts is worth it.
5. Always remember that the use of keyboard shortcuts keeps people healthy while performing computer activities.

5.2 How To Learn New Shortcut Keys

1. Do a research on them: quick references (a cheat sheet comprehensively compiled like ours) can go a long way to help you improve.
2. Buy applications that show you keyboard shortcuts every time you execute an action with mouse.
3. Disconnect your mouse if you must learn this fast.
4. Read user manuals and help topics (Whether offline or online).

5.3 Your Reward For Knowing Shortcut Keys.

1. You will get faster unimaginably.
2. Your level of efficiency will increase.
3. You will find it easy to use.
4. Opportunities are high that you will become an expert in what you do.
5. You won't have to go for **Office button**, click **New,** click **Blank and Recent**, and click **Create** just to insert a fresh/blank page. **Ctrl +N** takes care of that in a second.

A Funny Note: Keyboarding and Mousing are in a marital union with Keyboarding being the head, so it will be unfair for anybody to put asunder between them.

5.4 Why We Emphasize On The Use of Shortcuts.

You may never leave your mouse completely unless you are ready to make your brain a box of keyboard shortcuts which will really be frustrating, just imagine yourself learning all shortcuts that go with the programs you use and their various versions. You shouldn't learn keyboard shortcuts that way.

Why we are emphasizing on the use of shortcuts is because mouse usage is becoming unusually common and unhealthy, too. So we just want to make sure both are combined so you can get fast, productive and healthy in your computer activities. All you need to know is just the most important ones associated with the programs you use.

CHAPTER 2.

15 (Fifteen) Special Keyboard Shortcuts.

The fifteen special keyboard shortcuts are fifteen (15) shortcuts every computer user should know.

The following is a list of keyboard shortcuts every computer user should know:

1. **Ctrl + A:** Control A, highlights or selects everything you have in the environment where you are working.

   > *If you are like **"Wow, the content of this document is large and there is no time to select all of it, besides, it's going to mount pressure on my computer?"** Using the mouse for this is an outdated method of handling a task like selecting all, Ctrl+A will take care of that in a second.*

2. **Ctrl + C:** Control C copies any highlighted or selected element within the work environment.

    Saves the time and stress which would have been used to right click and click again just to copy. Use ctrl+c.

3. **Ctrl + N:** Control N opens a new window or file.

    Instead of clicking **File**, **New**, **blank/ template** *and another* **click**, *just press* ***Ctrl + N*** *and a fresh page or window will* appear instantly.

4. **Ctrl + O:** Control O opens a new program.

    Use ctrl +O when you want to locate / open a file or program.

5. **Ctrl + P:** Control P prints the active document.

    Always use this to locate the printer dialog box, and thereafter print.

6. **Ctrl + S:** Control S saves a new document or file and changes made by the user.

    Please stop! Don't use the mouse. Just press Ctrl+S and everything will be saved.

7. **Ctrl +V:** Control V pastes copied elements into the active area of the program in use.

Using ctrl+V in a case like this Saves the time and stress of right clicking and clicking again just to paste.

8. **Ctrl + W:** Control W is used to close the page you are working on when you want to leave the work environment.

    "There is a way Debby does this without using the mouse. Oh my God, why didn't I learn it then?" Don't worry, I have the answer. Debby presses Ctrl+W to close active windows.

9. **Ctrl + X:** Control X cuts elements (making the elements to disappear from their original place). The difference between cutting and deleting elements is that in Cutting, what was cut doesn't get lost permanently but prepares itself so that it can be pasted on another location defined by the user.

    Use ctrl+x when you think ***"this shouldn't be here and I can't stand the stress of retyping or redesigning it on the rightful place it belongs".***

10. **Ctrl + Y:** Control Y undoes already done actions.

    Ctrl+Z brought back what you didn't need? Press Ctrl+ Y to remove it again.

11. **Ctrl + Z:** Control Z redoes actions.
    Can't find what you typed now or a picture you inserted, it suddenly disappeared or you mistakenly removed it? Press Ctrl+Z to bring it back.

12. **Alt + F4:** Alternative F4 closes active windows or items.

    *You don't need to move the mouse in order to close an active window, just press **Alt + F4**. Also use it when you are done or you don't want somebody who is coming to see what you are doing.*

13. **Ctrl + F6:** Control F6 Navigates between open windows, making it possible for a user to see what is happening in windows that are active.
    Are you working in Microsoft Word and want to find out if the other active window where your browser is loading a page is still progressing? Use Ctrl + F6.

14. **F1:** This displays the help window.

    *Is your computer malfunctioning? Use **F1** to find help when you don't know what next to do.*

15. **F12:** This enables user to make changes to an already saved document.

> *F12 is the shortcut to use when you want to change the format in which you saved your existing document, password it, change its name, change the file location or destination, or make other changes to it. It will save you time.*

Note: The Control (Ctrl) key on Windows and Linux operating system is the same thing as Command (Cmmd) key on a Macintosh computer. So if you replace Control with Command key on a Mac computer for the special shortcuts listed above, you will get the same result.

CHAPTER 3.

Keyboard Shortcuts for use in Adobe Acrobat DC.

About the application: This is an application developed by Adobe that is used by readers to create, view, manipulate, print, and manage Portable Document Format (PDF) files.

A fresh topic ⌐↳

Keyboard Shortcuts in Adobe Acrobat DC.

Note:

This topic provides instructions for Acrobat DC. If you're using Acrobat Reader DC, see <u>What can I do with Adobe Reader</u>. If you're using Acrobat XI, see <u>Acrobat XI Help</u>.

Keys for Selecting Tools.

To enable single-key shortcuts, open the Preferences dialog box, and under General, select the Use Single-Key Accelerators To Access Tools option.

Use the following list of keyboard shortcuts to enhance your productivity in Adobe Acrobat Reader.

Tool	Windows/UN IX Shortcut	Mac OS Shortcut
Hand tool	H	H
Temporarily select Hand tool	Spacebar	Spacebar
Select tool	V	V
Marquee Zoom tool	Z	Z
Cycle through zoom tools: Marquee Zoom,Dynamic Zoom, Loupe	Shift+Z	Shift+Z
Temporarily select Dynamic Zoom tool (when Marquee Zoom tool is selected)	Shift	Shift

Temporarily zoom out (when Marquee Zoom tool is selected)	Ctrl	Option
Temporarily select Zoom In tool	Ctrl+spacebar	Spacebar+Command
Select Object tool	R	R
Edit Object tool	O	O
Enter/Exit Forms editing	A	A
Crop tool	C	C
Link tool	L	L
Text Field tool	F	F
Cycle through tools in forms authoring mode: Text Field, Check Box, Radio Button, List Box, Dropdown Box, Button,	Shift+F	Shift+F

Digital Signature, Barcode		
3D tool	M	M
Cycle through Multimedia tools: 3D object, SWF, Sound, Video	Shift+M	Shift+M
Edit Document Text tool	T	T
Redaction	Shift+Y	Shift+Y
Cycle through Touch Up tools: Touch Up Text, Touch Up Reading Order, Touch Up Object	Shift+T	Shift+T
JavaScript Debugger	Ctrl+J	Command+J
Insert Blank Pages tool	Shift+Ctrl+T	Shift+Command+T
Insert Files	Ctrl+Shift+I	Shift+Command+I

Delete pages	Ctrl+Shift+D	
		Shift+Command+ D
Open Output Preview	~	~
Touch Up Reading Order tool (or if already selected, return focus to dialog box)	Shift+Ctrl+U	Shift+Command+ U

Keys for Working with Comments.

To enable single-key shortcuts, select the Use Single-Key Accelerators To Access Tools option in General preferences.

Result	Windows/UNI X Shortcut	Mac OS Shortcu t
Sticky Note tool	S	S
Text Edits tool	E	E
Stamp tool	K	K
Current highlighting tool	U	U
Cycle through highlighting tools: Highlighter,Underlin	Shift+U (Windows only)	Shift+U

e Text, Cross Out Text		
Current drawing markup tool	D	D
Cycle through drawing markup tools: Cloud, Arrow, Line, Rectangle, Oval, Polygon Line, Polygon, Pencil Tool, Eraser Tool	Shift+D (Windows only)	Shift+D
Cloud tool	Q (Windows only)	Q
Text Box tool	X	X
Current Stamp or Attach tool	J	J
Cycle through Stamp, Attach File, Record Audio Comment	Shift+J	Shift+J
Move focus to next comment or form field	Tab	Tab
Move focus to previous comment or form field	Shift+Tab	Shift+Tab
Open pop-up note (or text field in Comments List) for comment that has focus	Enter	Return

Closes pop-up (or text field in Comments List) for comment that has focus	Esc	Esc

Keys for Navigating a PDF.

Result	Windows/UNIX Shortcut	Mac OS Shortcut
Previous screen	Page Up or Shift+Enter	Page Up or Shift+Return
Next screen	Page Down or Enter	Page Down or Return
First page	Home or Shift+Ctrl+Page Up or Shift+Ctrl+Up Arrow	Home or Shift+Command+Up Arrow
Last page	End or Shift+Ctrl+Page Down or Shift+Ctrl+Down Arrow	End or Shift+Command+Down Arrow
Previous page	Left Arrow or Ctrl+Page Up	Left Arrow or Command+Page Up
Next page	Right Arrow or Ctrl+Page Down	Right Arrow or Command+Page Down

Previous open document	Ctrl+F6 (UNIX)	Command+F6
Next open document	Shift+Ctrl+F6 (UNIX)	Shift+Command+F6
Scroll up	Up Arrow	Up Arrow
Scroll down	Down Arrow	Down Arrow
Scroll (when Hand tool is selected)	Spacebar	Spacebar
Zoom in	Ctrl+equal sign	Command+equal sign
Zoom out	Ctrl+hyphen	Command+hyphen

Keys for Working with Forms.

Result	Windows/UNIX Shortcut	Mac OS Shortcut
Toggle between editing and previewing your form	P	P
Toggle Guides On / Off	G	G

Align selected fields left	L	L
Align selected fields right	R	R
Align selected fields top	T	T
Align selected fields bottom	B	B
Align selected fields horizontal	H	H
Align selected fields vertical	V	V
Center fields horizontally	Shift+H	Shift+H
Center fields vertically	Shift+V	Shift+V
Highlight fields	Shift+L	Shift+L
Show Tab Order	Shift+N	Shift+N
Document JavaScripts	Shift+D	Shift+D

Keys for Working with PDF Portfolios.

These keys are available in the files list of the Details pane.

Result	Windows Shortcut	Mac OS Shortcut
Move focus to the next or	Up Arrow or Down Arrow	Up Arrow or Down Arrow

previous row when in the body of the file list on the left		
If pressed in the body of the file list, navigate one level up from within a folder	Backspace	Delete
Press the Go Back button in a folder if focus is on the button.	Enter or Spacebar	Enter or Spacebar
If pressed when focus is on a row in the file list representing a subfolder, navigate to a subfolder, or open an attachment in Preview mode.	Enter	Enter
If in the body of the file	Home or End	Home or End

list, move to the first or last row		
If in the body of the file list, move to the next or last set of rows to fit the screen	Page Down or Page Up	Page Down or Page Up
Select or deselect all files	Ctrl+A or Shift+Ctrl+A	Command+A or Shift+Command+A
If in the body of the file list, extend the selection by adding the next row above or below the selected row	Shift+Up Arrow or Shift+Down Arrow	Shift+Up Arrow or Shift+Down Arrow
Change whether the row with focus is in the selection	Ctrl+Spacebar	Command+Spacebar
Move focus up or down one row without	Ctrl+Up Arrow or Ctrl+Down Arrow	Command+Up Arrow or Command+Down Arrow

changing the selection		

Keys for Navigating Task Panes.

Result	Windows Shortcut	Mac OS Shortcut
Move focus to the next item among Document pane, Task panes, Message bar, and Navigation bar	F6	F6
Move focus to the previous item among Document pane, Task panes, message bar, and Navigation bar	Shift+F6	Shift+F6
Move focus to the next panel in the Task pane	Ctrl+Tab	Option +Tab
Move focus to the previous panel in the Task pane	Ctrl+Shift+Tab	Command+ Shift+Tab
Navigate to the next panel and panel control within an open Task pane	Tab	Tab

Navigate to the previous panel and panel control within an open Task pane	Shift+Tab	Shift+Tab
Navigate to the next command button within a panel	Down Arrow	Down Arrow
Navigate to the previous command button within a panel	Up Arrow	Up Arrow
Expand or collapse panel in focus (press F6 to move focus to Tools pane, then tab to desired panel)	Spacebar or Enter	Spacebar or Enter
Open or close the Task pane	Shift+F4	Shift+F4
Close the pane that lists the tasks of an Action	Ctrl+Shift+F4	Ctrl+Shift+F4
Open the menu and move the focus to the first menu option when focus is on a command with a	Spacebar or Enter	Spacebar or Enter

submenu or submenu element with a flyout		
Move the focus back to the parent command button with a submenu or submenu element with a flyout	Esc	Esc
Run the command in focus	Spacebar or Enter	Spacebar or Enter
Navigate to the next item in the active panel in the Create New Action, Edit Action, Create Custom Tool, or the Edit Custom Tool dialog boxes	Tab	Tab
Navigate to the previous item in the active panel in the Create New Action, Edit Action, Create Custom Tool, or the Edit Custom Tool dialog boxes	Shift+Tab	Shift+Tab

Keys for General Navigation.

Result	Windows/UNIX Shortcut	Mac OS Shortcut
Move focus to menus (Windows, UNIX); expand first menu item (UNIX)	F10	Control+F2
Move focus to toolbar in browser and application (In application, sets focus to the first button in the top bar - Home)	Shift+F8	Shift+F8

Navigate through the other controls in the top bar - Home, Tools, Document	Right/Left Arrow or Tab/Shift Tab	Right/Left Arrow or Tab/Shift Tab
Select a highlighted control in the top bar	Enter or Spacebar	Return or Spacebar
Move to next open document tab (when multiple documents are open in same window)	Ctrl+Tab	Control+Tab
Move to previous open document tab (when multiple documents are open	Ctrl+Shift+Tab	Control+Shift+Tab

in same window)		
Move to next open document window (when focus is on document pane)	Ctrl+F6	Command+F6
Move to previous open document window (when focus is on document pane)	Ctrl+Shift+F6	Command+Shift+F6
Close current document	Ctrl+F4	Command+F4
Close all open documents	Not available	Command+Option+W
Move focus to next comment, link, or	Tab	Tab

form field in the document pane		
Move focus to document pane	F5	F5
Move focus to previous comment, link, or form field in the document pane	Shift+Tab	Shift+Tab
Activate selected tool, item (such as a movie clip or bookmark), or command	Spacebar or Enter	Spacebar or Return
Open context menu	Shift+F10	Control+click

Close context menu	F10	Esc
Return to Hand tool or Select tool	Esc	Esc
Move focus to next tab in a tabbed dialog box	Ctrl+Tab	Not available
Move to previous search result and highlight it in the document	Shift + F3 or Ctrl + Shift + G	Shift + Command + G
Move to next search result and highlight it in the document	F3 or Ctrl + G	Command + G
Search previous document (with Search	Alt+Shift+Left Arrow (Windows only)	Command+Shift+Left Arrow

results displaying multiple files)		
Search next document (with Search results displaying multiple files)	Alt+Shift+Right Arrow (Windows only)	Command+Shift+Ri ght Arrow
Select text (with Select tool selected)	Shift+arrow keys	Shift+arrow keys
Select next word or deselect previous word (with Select tool selected)	Shift+Ctrl+Righ t Arrow or Left Arrow	Not available

Keys for Working with Navigation Panels.

Result	Windows/UNI X Shortcut	Mac OS Shortcut

Open and move focus to navigation pane	Ctrl+Shift+F5	Command+Shift+F5
Move focus among the document, message bar, and navigation panels	F6	F6
Move focus to previous pane or panel	Shift+F6	Shift+F6
Move among the elements of the active navigation panel	Tab	Tab
Move to previous or next navigation panel and make it	Up Arrow or Down Arrow	Up Arrow or Down Arrow

active (when focus is on the panel button)		
Move to next navigation panel and make it active (when focus is anywhere in the navigation pane)	Ctrl+Tab	Not available
Expand the current bookmark (focus on Bookmark s panel)	Right Arrow or Shift+plus sign	Right Arrow or Shift+plus sign
Collapse the current bookmark (focus on Bookmark s panel)	Left Arrow or minus sign	Left Arrow or minus sign

Expand all bookmarks	Shift+*	Shift+*
Collapse selected bookmark	Forward Slash (/)	Forward Slash (/)
Move focus to next item in a navigation panel	Down Arrow	Down Arrow
Move focus to previous item in a navigation panel	Up Arrow	Up Arrow

Keys for Navigating the Help Window.

Result	Windows/UNIX Shortcut	Mac OS Shortcut
Open Help window	F1	F1 or Command+?
Close Help window	Ctrl+W (Windows only) or Alt+F4	Command+W
Move back to previously	Alt+Left Arrow	Command+Left Arrow

opened topic		
Move forward to next topic	Alt+Right Arrow	Command+Right Arrow
Move to next pane	Ctrl+Tab	See Help for your default browser
Move to previous pane	Shift+Ctrl+Tab	See Help for your default browser
Move focus to the next link within a pane	Tab	Not available
Move focus to the previous link within a pane	Shift+Tab	Not available
Activate highlighted link	Enter	Not available
Print Help topic	Ctrl+P	Command+P

Keys for Accessibility.

Result	Windows Shortcut	Mac OS Shortcut

Change reading settings for the current document	Shift+Ctrl+5	Shift+Command+5
Reflow a tagged PDF, and return to unreflowed view	Ctrl+4	Command+4
Activate and deactivate Read Out Loud	Shift+Ctrl+Y	Shift+Command+Y
Read only the current page out loud	Shift+Ctrl+V	Shift+Command+V
Read out loud from the current page to the end of the document	Shift+Ctrl+B	Shift+Command+B
Pause reading out loud	Shift+Ctrl+C	Shift+Command+C
Stop reading out loud	Shift+Ctrl+E	Shift+Command+E

Applies to: *Adobe Acrobat DC.*

Customer's Page.

This page is for customers who enjoyed Adobe Acrobat DC Keyboard Shortcuts.

Our beloved and respectable reader, we thank you very much for your patronage. Please we will appreciate it more if you rate and review this book; that is if it was helpful to you. Thank you.

Download Our EBooks Today For Free.

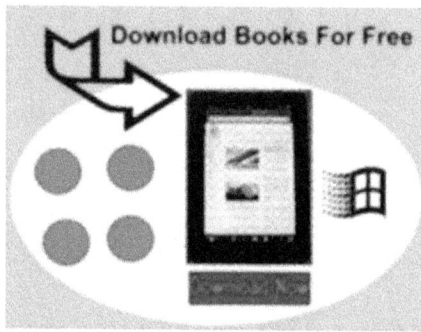

In order to appreciate our customers, we have made some of our titles available at 0.00. They are totally free. Feel free to get a copy of the free titles.

Here are books we give to our customers free of charge:

(A) For Keyboard Shortcuts in Windows check:

Windows 7 Keyboard Shortcuts.

(B) For Keyboard Shortcuts in Office 2016 for Windows check:

Word 2016 Keyboard Shortcuts For Windows.

(C) For Keyboard Shortcuts in Office 2016 for Mac check:

OneNote 2016 Keyboard Shortcuts For Macintosh.

Follow this link to download any of the titles listed above for free.

Note: Feel free to download them from our website or your favorite bookstore today. Thank you.

Other Books By This Publisher.

Titles for single programs under Shortcut Matters Series are not part of this list.

S/N	Title	Series
Series A: Limits Breaking Quotes.		
1	Discover Your Key Christian Quotes	Limits Breaking Quotes
Series B: Shortcut Matters.		
1	Windows 7 Shortcuts	Shortcut Matters
2	Windows 7 Shortcuts & Tips	Shortcut Matters
3	Windows 8.1 Shortcuts	Shortcut Matters
4	Windows 10 Shortcut Keys	Shortcut Matters
5	Microsoft Office 2007 Keyboard Shortcuts For Windows.	Shortcut Matters
6	Microsoft Office 2010 Shortcuts For Windows.	Shortcut Matters
7	Microsoft Office 2013 Shortcuts For Windows.	Shortcut Matters
8	Microsoft Office 2016 Shortcuts For Windows.	Shortcut Matters
9	Microsoft Office 2016 Keyboard Shortcuts For Macintosh.	Shortcut Matters
10	Top 11 Adobe Programs Keyboard Shortcuts	Shortcut Matters
11	Top 10 Email Service Providers Keyboard Shortcuts	Shortcut Matters
12	Hot Corel Programs Keyboard Shortcuts	Shortcut Matters

13	Top 10 Browsers Keyboard Shortcuts	Shortcut Matters
14	Microsoft Browsers Keyboard Shortcuts.	Shortcut Matters
15	Popular Email Service Providers Keyboard Shortcuts	Shortcut Matters
16	Professional Video Editing with Keyboard Shortcuts.	Shortcut Matters
17	Popular Web Browsers Keyboard Shortcuts.	Shortcut Matters

Series C: Teach Yourself.

1	Teach Yourself Computer Fundamentals	Teach Yourself
2	Teach Yourself Computer Fundamentals Workbook	Teach Yourself

Series D: For Painless Publishing

1	Self-Publish it with CreateSpace.	For Painless Publishing
2	Where is my money? Now solved for Kindle and CreateSpace	For Painless Publishing
3	Describe it on Amazon	For Painless Publishing

www.ingramcontent.com/pod-product-compliance
Lightning Source LLC
Chambersburg PA
CBHW071813170526
45167CB00003B/1299

* 9 7 8 1 5 4 3 2 2 8 4 2 7 *